General Information

Introduction

This book was written with the use of Hoffman Fabrics Bali Pops in mind. Each Bali Pop contains 40 luscious 2 ½" strips of Hoffman Bali Batik fabrics. The strips range in value from light to dark, with the difference in value being narrower than what you might expect to find in traditional printed fabrics.

While all of the quilts in this book were made using the cut strip sets, you can easily substitute 40 - 2 ½" strips from your own fabric stash. If you wish to achieve similar results, take a few minutes to study the fabrics in the quilt you plan to make to determine how to select fabrics.

Dynamic Duos!

When I began designing quilts to use Hoffman Fabrics Bali Pops, I wondered if I would find them interesting to use, or if I would be disappointed because I didn't have the opportunity to select the fabrics myself. The quilt plans were drawn up and I sat down at my trusty sewing machine to sew.

Wow, did I ever have fun! What a liberation! The construction process went so smoothly because the preliminary cutting was already done. WooHoo!

After completing the first quilt for Strip Therapy, I found myself unable to put the fabrics away. I immediately began playing with the leftover tidbits of fabric and constructed a smaller quilt.

When piecing quilts, I cut the fabric conservatively. I remove as little as possible, when it is necessary to trim the strip ends. This approach leaves the largest scraps at the end of a piecing project. These scraps are then trimmed and sewn together to create the second, much smaller quilt.

As you page through this book, you will see that the patterns are color coded. For example, the two quilts on the green pages can be made from a single Bali Pop with the addition of an accent fabric and a final border fabric.

Because the bonus quilts are made using pieces that would normally be discarded, and everyone's idea of "conservative" cutting is different, your bonus quilt might not be the same size as the sample quilt. The instructions given are just a guideline for the construction of your bonus quilt.

Basics

* All quilt patterns have been written specifically with the use of 2 ½" strips from Hoffman Fabrics Bali Pops collection in mind. Cutting and sewing instructions reflect this.

* Yardage is calculated on 42" wide fabric. Binding and border strips are cut the width of fabric - WOF. Final borders are cut the length of the fabric.

* Fabric value is relative. Many of the following patterns instruct you to divide the fabric strips into light and dark groupings. Some of the strips can be logically placed into either of the piles. Because the Bali Pop collections tend to be fairly low contrast, you will need to make a judgement call. There is no right or wrong decision.

* Additional basic piecing directions can be found on our website.

Pressing

* FINGER PRESS!!! All seams are finger pressed, including seams between long strips.

* Press each seam as directed. To the best of my ability, I have tried to find the most efficient pressing for each pattern. The seams will be pressed in opposite directions or open to reduce bulk. If no pressing directions are given, press as you wish.

* A great steam iron is a wonderful tool if used judiciously! Many use the iron with too much gusto. When piecing, I finger press all seams until the block is complete. Only after the final seams are finger pressed do I press with a iron in a straight up and down motion! This prevents stretching and distortion of the block.

Spinsanity

Jots and Tiddles

Spinsanity

Finished Size: 66" x 74"

40 - 8" blocks

Fabric Requirements and Cutting Instructions:

Bali Pop ~ Kiwiberry   1 roll of 40 - 2 ½" strips

Black   (1895/4 Black)   2 ¼ yards
  20 strips 2 ½" x wof - block construction
  1 strip 11" x 2 ½"
  First Border 6 strips 2 ½" x wof

Corner Triangles (1895/276 Sea Urchin)   ¼ yard
  1 square 7" - cut twice diagonally
  1 strip 4 ½" x 11"

Accent   (OA-C143/115 Grass)   1 ¼ yards
  Second Border - cut 6 strips 1 ½" x wof
  Binding - 7 strips 2" x wof

Final Border (E257/136 Peacock)   2 yards
  4 strips 6 ½" x 69" lengthwise cut
  1 square 10 5/8" cut once diagonally

Backing   72" x 80"   4 yards

Block Construction

1. Sort the 2 ½" strips into pairs of contrasting fabrics. Good contrast will produce the secondary pattern.

2. Stitch the strip pairs together along the long edge. Stitch a black strip to the second long edge of the light strip. Press all seams open to reduce bulk.

3. Cut the sewn/pressed strips into 4 ½" squares as diagramed below, using the template on the next page. Place the lines at the middle of the template along the seam lines of the sewn strip. Each strip will yield 8 squares. (The diagram blue represents the black fabric.) Please read the NOTES at right before sub-cutting the strips.

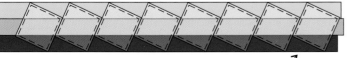

Make 20 strip sets.   Black

NOTE When cutting squares, start from the "jagged" end of the sewn strip (see diagram at lower left). This is the most efficient use of the sewn strip - and will allow the largest leftover strip scrap for use in the Jots and Tiddles quilt on page 7.

CUTTING NOTE

Not all strips may be cut perfectly 2 ½" wide, and all seam allowances may not be exact. So a few of you, myself included, may need to fudge when cutting the sewn strips into squares. If it is not possible to place the lines on the interior of the template exactly on the sew seamlines, then place the two points marked by an "x" precisely on the seam line, while allowing the remainder of the drawn line to stray from the sewn seam. Although this may tweak the angle of the light strip slightly, it will place the star points exactly where you want them when the blocks are sewn together.

4. Sew the cut squares into blocks as diagramed below. The squares from each strip set will yield 2 blocks that measure 8 ½" when measured raw edge to raw edge. Press seams open to reduce bulk. Make a total of 40 blocks.

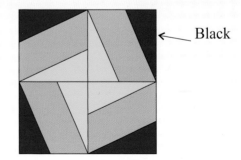

← Black

5. Stitch the 11" x 4 ½" strip of light corner fabric to the 11" x 2 ½" strip of black fabric. Press the seam open. Cut two squares from the sewn/pressed strip using the square template.

5

6. Stitch a 7" quarter square triangle to two sides of the squares from step 5. Press the seams open. Make 2.

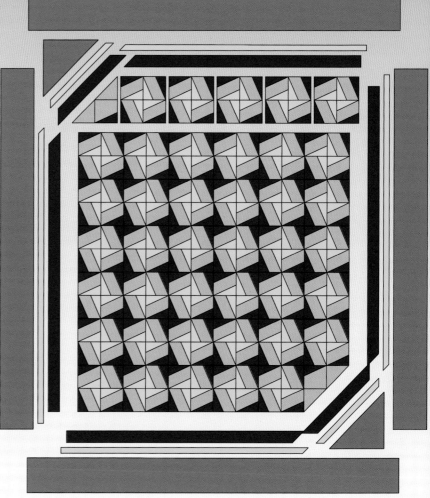

Quilt Top Assembly

1. Arrange blocks as diagramed at right - into 7 rows of 6 blocks - placing the corner units at the upper left and lower right. Stitch rows together. Press all seams open to reduce bulk.

2. Stitch first border strips together using diagonal seaming. Cut borders to length. Attach side borders first and then the top and bottom borders. Press all seams toward the border strips. Trim the corner as diagramed and attach the first border strip along the diagonal edge of the corner block. Press toward the border strip. Trim strip ends.

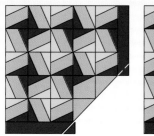 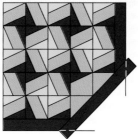

3. In the same manner, apply the second border of accent fabric. Press all seams toward the accent fabric border.

4. Stitch a 10 5/8" half square triangle of Final Border Fabric to the two diagonal corners. Press the seams toward the triangle.

5. Trim the final borders strips to length as needed. Attach side borders first and then the top and bottom borders. Press all seams toward the final border strips.

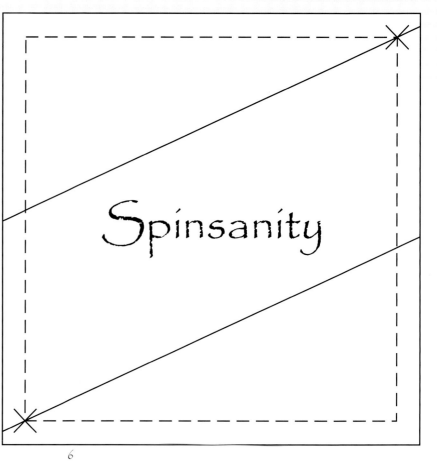

Spinsanity

Jots and Tiddles

Finished Size: 22" x 29"

Cutting Instructions:

Black   (1895/4 Black)
First Border and Sash 3 strips 1 ½" x wof

Accent   (OA-C143/115 Grass)
Second Border - cut 2 strips 1 ½" x wof
Binding - 3 strips 2" x wof

Final Border   (E257/136 Peacock)
2 strips 2 ½" x 29"
2 strips 2 ½" x 26"

Scrap Quilt Construction

1. Start with the scrap wedges left from the sub-cutting of the Pinwheel quilt. Carefully remove and discard the black accent piece from the sewn strip. Press the scrap wedge to flatten the former seam.

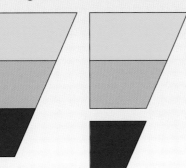

2. Stitch pairs of scrap wedges together along the diagonal edge. Press seams open. This will yield 10 units. These units will vary in length.

3. Measure the sewn units. Remove the longest unit from the pile and reserve for step 4. Trim the remaining 9 units to the length of the shortest unit - my shortest unit measured 6 ¾" long.

4. Trim the ends of the longest strip, reserved in step 3. Cut this unit into 3 equal pieces.

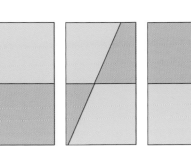

Quilt Top Assembly

1. Arrange the units from step 3 into 3 vertical columns of 3 units. Add a partial unit from step 4 to each of the 3 columns. Stitch the columns together and press all seams open.

2. Cut sashing/border strips to needed lengths and stitch to quilt. Apply black strips first, then accent strips, and finish with the final border.

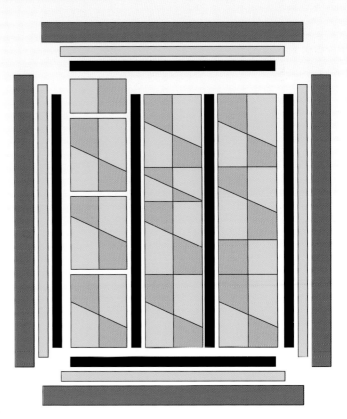

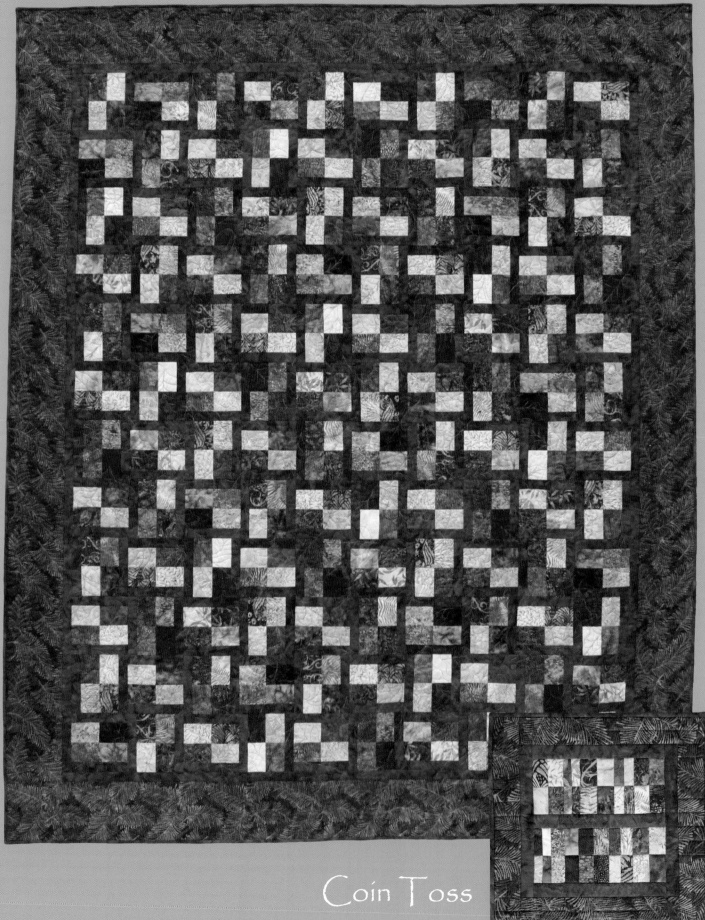

Coin Toss

Fuzzy Logic

Finished Size: 74" x 86"

120 blocks - 6"

Fabric Requirements and Cutting Instructions:

Bali Pop ~ Mint Chip   1 roll of 40 ~ 2 ½" strips

Accent Fabric (1895/358 Vegas)   3 yards
   Cut 40 strips 1 ½" x wof
      subcut strips into 240 rectangles 1 ½" x 6 ½"
   First Border 7 strips 1 ½" x wof
   Binding - 8 strips 2" x wof

Final Border   2 ½ yards
   4 strips 6 ½"x 78" lengthwise cut

Backing   80" x 92"   5 ½ yards

Block Construction

1. Sort the 2 ½" strips into pairs - one light and one dark strip.

2. Stitch the strip pairs together as diagramed below along the long edges. Press the seams toward the Dark fabric strips. Cut sewn strip sets into 3 ½" segments. Each sewn strip set will yield 12 segments. Reserve the remainder of the strips left after cutting the segments for the Coin Toss quilt on page 10.

←3 ½"→

3. Stitch the segments from step 2 together as diagramed below. Press the seam in one direction.

4. To each long edge of the rectangle stitch a 1 ½" x 6 ½" rectangle of Accent Fabric. Press the seams toward the accent strips. Completed block will measure 6 ½"
raw edge to
raw edge.
Make 120 blocks.

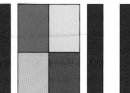

Quilt Top Assembly

1. Arrange blocks as diagramed below - into 10 rows of 12 blocks - watch the placement of the blocks and the creation of the secondary pattern. Stitch blocks into rows. Press all seams toward the accent strips.

2. Stitch the rows together. Press seams in one direction.

3. Stitch first border strips together using diagonal seaming. Cut borders to length. Attach side borders first and then the top and bottom borders. Press all seams toward the border strips.

4. Trim the final borders strips to length as needed. Attach side borders first and then the top and bottom borders. Press all seams toward the final border strips.

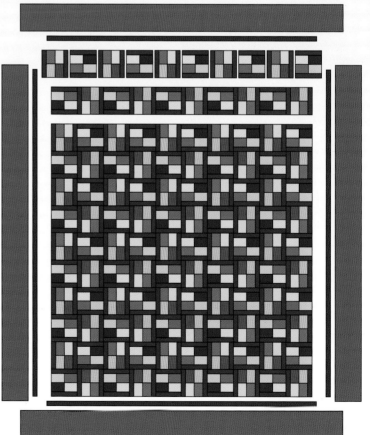

Coin Toss

Finished Size: 16" x 15"

Cutting Instructions:

Accent Fabric (1895/358 Vegas)

First Border and Sash - 2 strips 1 ½" x wof
Binding - 2 strips 2" x wof

Final Border

2 strips 2 ½" x wof

Scrap Quilt Construction

1. Start with the scrap segments left from the sub-cutting of the Fuzzy Logic quilt. Trim the selvedge end the amount necessary to clean up the end of the segment. Do not pay any attention to segment width, because they will naturally vary.

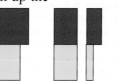

2. Stitch the coin segments into two rows of 10 coin segments each. Arrange the segments in such a way as to create two rows about equal in length. Stitch the coin pairs together as diagramed below. Press the seams in one direction.

3. Trim the longer strip if necessary to make the strips the same length.

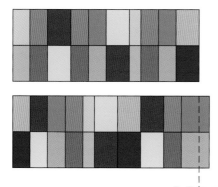

Quilt Top Assembly

1. Cut sashing/border strips to neede length and stitch to the quilt. Press all seams toward the sashing/border strips

2. Cut final border strips to needed length and stitch to quilt. Press all seams toward the final border strips.

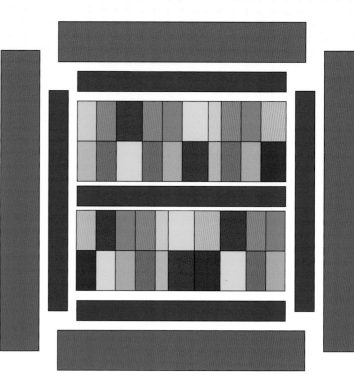

Mood Swing

Linda's Twist

Mood Swing

Finished Size: 62" x 70"

42 - 8" blocks

Fabric Requirements and Cutting Instructions:

Bali Pop - Strawberry Fields 1 roll of 40 - 2 ½" strips

First Border (C255/47-Gold)   1 ¼ yards
   1 strip 2 ½" x wof - block construction
   6 strips 1 ½" x wof
   Binding - 7 strips 2" x wof

Final Border (E245/346 Huckleberry)   2 yards
   1 strip 2 ½" x wof - block construction
   4 strips 6 ½" x 64" lengthwise cut

Backing   68" x 76"   4 yards

Block Construction

1. Sort the 40 Bali Pop strips and the 2 ½" strips of First Border and Final Border fabric into pairs. Good contrast will produce the secondary pattern.

2. Stitch the strip pairs together along the long edge. Press all seams open to reduce bulk.

3. Cut the sewn/pressed strips into triangles as diagramed below using the Mood Swing template on page 23. Place the line at the middle of the template along the seamline of the sewn strip. (I used a large triangle ruler to facilitate the cutting process.) Each strip should yield 8 triangles. Reserve the strip scraps for Linda's Twist quilt on page 13.

4. Sew the cut triangles into blocks as diagramed at right. The triangles from each strip set will yield 2 blocks that measure 8 ½" when measured raw edge to raw edge. Press all seams open. Make a total of 42 blocks.

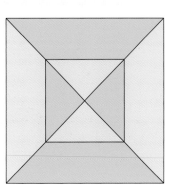

Quilt Top Assembly

1. Arrange blocks as diagramed below - into 7 rows of 6 blocks - watch the placement of the blocks and the creation of the secondary pattern. Stitch blocks into rows. Press all seams open.

2. Stitch the rows together. Press seams open.

3. Stitch first border strips together using diagonal seaming. Cut borders to needed length. Attach side borders first and then the top and bottom borders. Press all seams toward the border strips.

4. Trim the final borders strips to length as needed. Attach side borders first and then the top and bottom borders. Press all seams toward the final border strips.

Linda's Twist

Finished Size: 25" x 25"

Cutting Instructions:

First and Third Border   (C255/47-Gold)
  4 strips 1 ½" x wof
  Binding - 3 strips 2" x wof

Final Border   (E245/346 Huckleberry)
  4 strips 2 ½" x 28" - lengthwise cut

Scrap Quilt Construction

1. Start with the scrap segments left from the sub-cutting of the Mood Swing quilt. Trim the selvedge end as necessary. Trim just the amount necessary to clean up the end of the segment. Sort the segments into two groups. The shorter pieces, as shown on the left, will be set aside for construction of the second border strip. The longer pieces, as shown on the right, will be used in the construction of the quilt center panel.

2. Stitch the long segments together in pairs. Make a total of 8 pairs. Press the diagonal seams open. Join the pairs together to make 4 blocks. Press long seams open to reduce bulk.
Note the placement of the light trapezoid. This will create the center star.

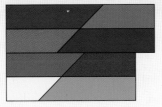

3. Join the 4 blocks together as diagramed below. Place the light trapezoids in the center to create the secondary star design. Trim the unit as necessary to square the block. Please notice that your star may not be centered due to the varied strip lengths.

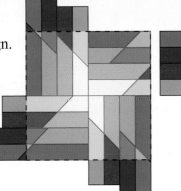

4. Cut first border strips to length. Attach side borders first and then the top and bottom borders. Press all seams toward the border strips.

5. Join the smaller scraps from step 1 together, trimming as necessary, and attach to edges of quilt top. If you run short of units, measure the pieced border strip and cut a strip of border fabric to fill the gap.

6. Cut third border strips to length. Attach side borders first and then the top and bottom borders. Press all seams toward the border strips.

7. Trim the final borders strips to length as needed. Attach side borders first and then the top and bottom borders. Press all seams toward the final border strips.

Psycho

Spin Cycle

Psycho

Finished Size: 62" x 70"

42 ~ 8" blocks

Fabric Requirements and Cutting Instructions:

Bali Pop ~ Sherbert   1 roll of 40 - 2 ½" strips

First Border (E209/111 Watermelon)   1 ¼ yards
  1 strip 2 ½" x wof - block construction
  6 strips 1 ½" x wof
  Binding - 7 strips 2" x wof

Final Border   (E257/120 Hyacinth)   2 yards
  1 strip 2 ½" x wof - block construction
  4 strips 6 ½" x 64" - lengthwise cut

Backing   68" x 76"   4 yards

Block Construction

1. Sort the 40 - 2 ½" strips into two sets - 20 light strips and 20 dark strips - remembering that value is relative. To the light set add a 2 ½" strip of First Border fabric. To the dark set add a 2 ½" strip of Final Border fabric.

2. Cut each of the 21 light strips into:
  a: 2 squares 2 ½"
  b: 2 rectangles 2 ½" x 4 ½"
  c: 2 rectangles 2 ½" x 6 ½"
  d: 1 rectangle 2 ½" x 8 ½"

Cut each of the 21 dark strips into:
  e: 2 squares 2 ½"
  f: 2 rectangles 2 ½" x 4 ½"
  g: 2 rectangles 2 ½" x 6 ½"
  h: 1 rectangle 2 ½" x 8 ½"

Reserve the scrap strip remnants for the construction of the Spin Cycle quilt on page 16.

3. Stitch the blocks together as diagramed below. Press all seams open.

Quilt Top Assembly

1. Arrange blocks as diagramed below - into 7 rows of 6 blocks - watch the placement of the blocks and the creation of the secondary pattern. Stitch blocks into rows. Press all seams open.

2. Stitch the rows together. Press seams open.

3. Stitch first border strips together using diagonal seaming. Cut borders to needed length. Attach side borders first and then the top and bottom borders. Press all seams toward the border strips.

4. Trim the final borders strips to length as needed. Attach side borders first and then the top and bottom borders. Press all seams toward the final border strips.

Make 21 Block A   Make 21 Block B

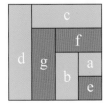 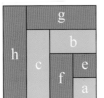

Spin Cycle

Finished Size: 24" x 48"

21 ~ 6" blocks

Cutting Instructions:

Accent Fabric   (1895/30 Lilac)   ½ yard
4 strips 2 ½" x wof

First Border   (E209/111 Watermelon)
1 strips 2 ½" x wof
Binding - 4 strips 2" x wof

Final Border   (E257/120 Hyacinth)
2 strips 2 ½" x 47"
2 strips 2 ½" x 27"

Block Construction

1. Sort the 42 strip remnants from the Psycho quilt according to length. Trim the shortest 21 pieces to 2 ½" x 6 ½". Cut the remaining 21 remnants into 42 trapezoids using the Spin Cycle template on page 23.

2. Cut the 2 ½" wide Accent Fabric strips into 42 trapezoids using the Spin Cycle template.

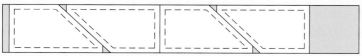

3. Stitch each Accent Fabric trapezoid to a Bali Pop Trapezoid. Press the seam open to reduce bulk.

4. Join the 42 trapezoid units to the 21- 2 ½" x 6 ½" Bali Pop strips. Press the seams toward the center strip.

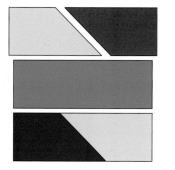
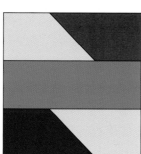

Quilt Top Assembly

1. Arrange blocks as diagramed below - into 7 rows of 3 blocks - watch the placement of the blocks and the creation of the secondary pattern. Stitch blocks into rows. Press all seams open.

2. Stitch the rows together. Press seams open.

3. Stitch first border strips together using diagonal seaming. Cut borders to needed length. Attach side borders first and then the top and bottom borders. Press all seams toward the border strips.

4. Trim the final borders strips to length as needed. Attach side borders first and then the top and bottom borders. Press all seams toward the final border strips.

Insomnia

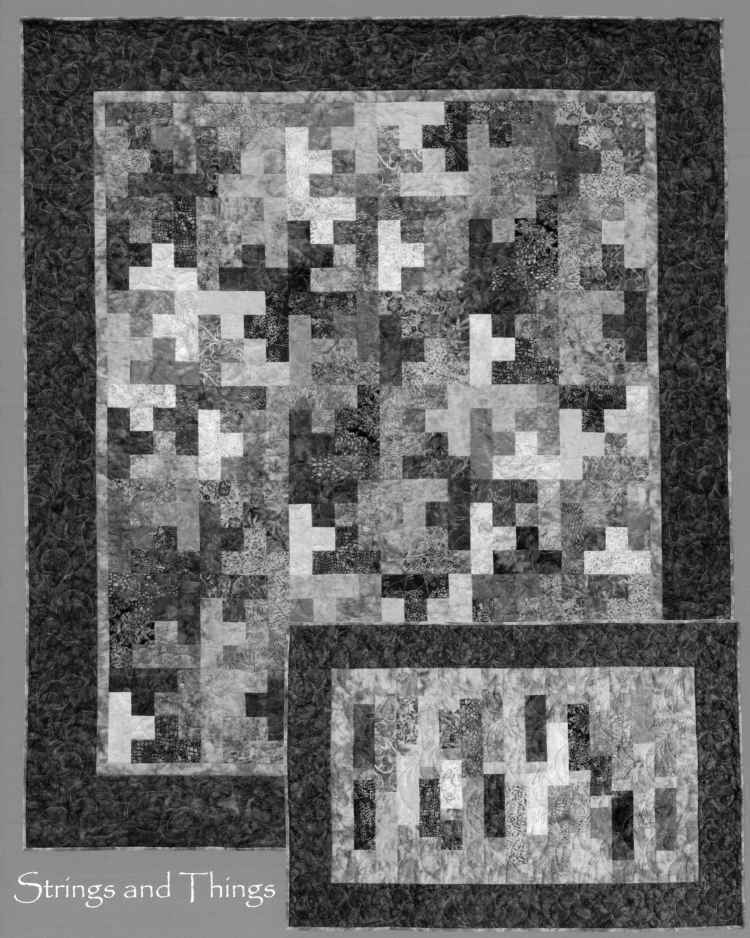

Strings and Things

Insomnia

Finished Size: 62" x 70"

42 - 8" blocks

Fabric Requirements and Cutting Instructions:

Bali Pop ~ Mulberry   1 roll of 40 - 2 ½" strips

First Border   (1895/293 Fox)   1 ½ yards
1 strip 2 ½" x wof - block construction
First Border - cut 6 strips 1 ½" x wof
Binding - 7 strips 2" x wof

Final Border   (E131/241 Sonoma)   2 yards
1 strip 2 ½" x wof - block construction
4 strips 6 ½" x 64" - lengthwise cut

Backing   68" x 76"   4 yards

Block Construction

1. Cut each of the 42 strips (Bali Pop strips + first and final border 2 ½" strips) into:
      4 squares 2 ½"
      4 rectangles 6 ½"

2. Select 4 fabrics per block. Stitch the four - 2 ½" squares together to make the 4 patch center. Press as desired. Make 42 - 4 patch units.

3. Arrange the four - 2 ½" x 6 ½" rectangles around the 4 patch as diagramed below. The first rectangle will be sewn using a partial seam. Align rectangle 1 with the corner of the 4 patch and sew from the corner to the center of the 4 patch (as indicated by the dark line). Finger press the seam toward the rectangle.

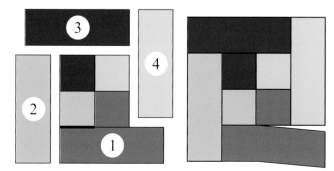

Add rectangles 2, 3 and 4, finger pressing each seam as it is sewn. Then complete the seam that attaches rectangle 1. Completed blocks will measure 8 ½" when measured raw edge to raw edge. Make 42 blocks.

Quilt Top Assembly

1. Arrange blocks as diagramed below - into 6 rows of 7 blocks. Stitch blocks together into rows. Press the seams in one direction.

2. Stitch the rows together. Press seams in one direction.

3. Stitch first border strips together using diagonal seaming. Cut borders to needed length. Attach side borders first and then the top and bottom borders. Press all seams toward the border strips.

4. Trim the final borders strips to length as needed. Attach side borders first and then the top and bottom borders. Press all seams toward the final border strips.

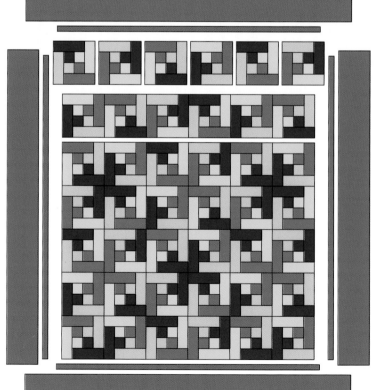

Strings and Things

Finished Size 27" x 42"

Cutting Instructions:

Accent Fabric   (1895-293 Fox)

 5 strips 2 ½" x wof

  Binding - 4 strips 2" x wof

Final Border   (E131-241 Sonoma)

 2 strips 4 ½" x 44" lengthwise cut

 2 strips 4 ½" x 24" lengthwise cut

Scrap Quilt Construction

1. Start with the scrap segments left from the sub-cutting of the Insomnia quilt. Trim the strips as necessary to square up the ends. Because the fabric pieces are not the same length, variation will naturally occur. My strip remnants ranged from 3" to 7 ½" in length.

2. Sub-cut Accent Fabric:

   Cut one strip into ~20 pieces 1 ½" x 2 ½"

3. Arrange the remnant strip segments from step 1 into a long column, 15 rows deep. Each row should contain 2 or 3 Bali Pop segments. Join the segments, separated with a 1 ½" x 2 ½" accent piece. Press the seams toward the gold accent fabric.

4. Attach 2 ½" wide strip segments cut from the accent strips to each end of the rows. Make the rows approximately the same length, staggering the placement of the 1 ½" wide accent pieces. Position a 2 ½" strip of accent fabric along the top and the bottom. Stitch the rows together. Press the long seams in one direction.

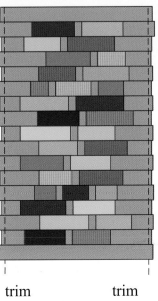

5. Trim the edges of the quilt top. My trimmed quilt width was 20".

trim   trim

Quilt Top Assembly

1. Cut border strips and stitch to quilt. Cut strips to length as needed. Attache top and bottom borders first and then side borders. Press all seams toward the final border strips.

Hot Flash

Melody's Madness

Hot Flash

Finished Size: 62" x 70"

42 - 8" blocks

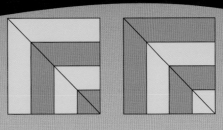

Make 21 Light
Make 21 Dark

Fabric Requirements and Cutting Instructions:

Bali Pop ~ Butterscotch   1 roll of 40 - 2 ½" strips

First Border   (839/112 Dawn)   1 ½ yards
  2 strips 2 ½" x wof - block construction
  6 strips 1 ½" x wof
  Binding - 7 strips 2" x wof

Final Border   (E230/389 Paprika)   2 yards
  2 strips 2 ½" x wof - block construction
  4 strips 6 ½" x 64" - lengthwise cut

Backing   68" x 76"   4 yards

Block Construction

1. Sort the 2 ½" strips into groups of four - each group made up of 2 light and 2 dark strips.

2. Stitch the strip together as diagramed below along the long edges. Press the seams open to distribute bulk.

3. Cut the sewn/pressed strips into triangles as diagramed below using the Hot Flash template on page 23. (I used a large triangle ruler to facilitate the cutting process.) Cut 4 triangles with the diagonal edge laying right to left and 4 left to right Each strip should yield 8 triangles - 4 right and 4 left. Reserve the strip scrap for Melody's Madness quilt on page 22.

4. Sew the cut triangles into blocks, assemble the units as diagramed above right. Press the seams open. Make 21 light blocks and 21 dark blocks.

Quilt Top Assembly

1. Arrange blocks as diagramed below - into 7 rows of 6 blocks - watch the placement of the blocks and the creation of the secondary pattern. Stitch blocks into rows. Press all seams open.

2. Stitch the rows together. Press seams open.

3.   Stitch first border strips together using diagonal seaming. Cut borders to needed length. Attach side borders first and then the top and bottom borders. Press all seams toward the border strips.

4. Trim the final borders strips to length as needed. Attach side borders first and then the top and bottom borders. Press all seams toward the final border strips.

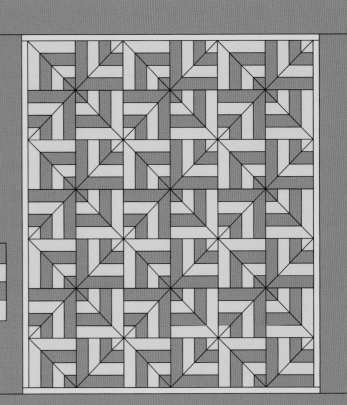

Melody's Madness

Finished Size: 33" x 39"

20 - 4" pieced blocks

Cutting Instructions:

First Border   (839/112 Dawn)

  2 strips 4 ½" x wof - subcut into 12 squares 4 ½"
  3 strips 1 ½" x wof
  Binding - 4 strips 2" x wof

Final Border   (E230/389 Paprika)

  3 squares 7" - cut twice diagonally - setting triangles
  2 squares 3 ¾" - cut once diagonally - corners
  2 strips 4 ½" x 34" - lengthwise cut
  2 strips 4 ½" x 36" - lengthwise cut

Scrap Quilt Construction

1. Arrange the remnants from the Hot Flash quilt as diagramed below. The light and dark edges of the segments are alternated to distribute the values across the created fabric.

2. Stitch the segments together. Press the seams open to distribute bulk.

3. Cut the sewn/pressed strips into 4 ½" squares as diagramed below using your rotary ruler (I used a 4 ½" square ruler to facilitate the cutting process.)

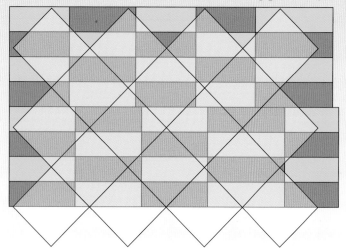

4. As you are cutting the 4 ½" squares, be judicious. All scrap pieces from the edges of the created fabric, are sewn together once again to create even more fabric to increase the yield of 4 ½" cut squares. I was able to get 20 squares, your yield may vary depending upon your thriftiness when cutting.

Quilt Top Assembly

1. Arrange blocks in diagonal rows. Separate the pieced blocks with 4 ½" squares of accent fabric. Place a final border fabric triangle at each end of the rows as diagramed below and sew. Press seams open.

2. Stitch the rows together. Press seams open.

3. Cut first border strips to needed length. Attach side borders first and then the top and bottom borders. Press all seams toward the border strips.

4. Trim the final borders strips to length as needed. Attach side borders first and then the top and bottom borders. Press all seams toward the final border strips.

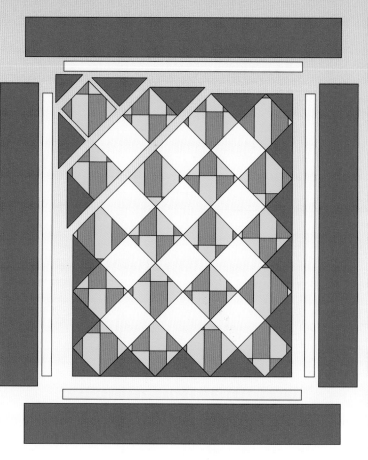